GREAT BRITAIN

Richard and Sheila Tames

FRANKLIN WATTS
LONDON • SYDNEY

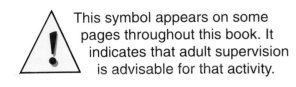
This symbol appears on some pages throughout this book. It indicates that adult supervision is advisable for that activity.

Revised and updated edition 2003

Franklin Watts
96 Leonard Street
London EC2A 4XD

Franklin Watts Australia
45-51 Huntley Street,
Alexandria, NSW 2015

Editor: Hazel Poole
Designer: Sally Boothroyd
Comissioned photography: Peter Millard
Artwork: Teri Gower
Picture research: Juliet Duff

A CIP catalogue record for this book is available from the British Library

ISBN   0 7496 4925 9

Printed in Dubai

CONTENTS

Introducing Great Britain

Hello and welcome to Great Britain. Before you start to explore, here is some useful information about the country to help you on your way.

FLYING THE FLAG

The Union flag (sometimes known as the Union Jack) was invented for use on royal ships in 1603 when England and Scotland began to be ruled by the same monarch. It originally combined the flags of England (a red cross on white) and Scotland (a diagonal white cross on dark blue). In 1801, a diagonal red cross on white was added for Ireland which was ruled by Britain at that time. Wales has its own separate flag of white and green bands with a red dragon.

GREAT BRITAIN IN THE WORLD

Great Britain is made up of three countries, England, Wales and Scotland. Great Britain and Northern Ireland make up the United Kingdom, along with various island groups such as the Scilly Isles, Hebrides, Shetland Islands and Orkney Islands. Great Britain covers an area of 229,979 square kilometres (England 130,439 sq km; Scotland 78,772 sq km; and Wales 20, 768 sq km). It lies in western Europe, surrounded by the Atlantic Ocean, Irish Sea, North Sea, and the English Channel. London is the capital of Great Britain, with Edinburgh and Cardiff the capital cities of Scotland and Wales respectively.

A DEMOCRATIC MONARCHY

Britain is a democratic monarchy. The head of state is Queen Elizabeth II. She is also head of the Commonwealth which unites over 50 countries that used to be governed by Britain.

Parliament is made up of two houses – the House of Commons and the House of Lords. The Prime Minister is the leader of the government.

GOD SAVE THE QUEEN

Britain was the first country in the world to have a national anthem. In its present form it dates from 1745. There is a separate Welsh national anthem – *Hen Wlad Fy Nhadau* (Land of My Fathers) – which dates from 1868. Although not a national anthem as such, Scots often sing "Flower of Scotland" on sporting occasions.

MONEY AND STAMPS

The basic unit of currency is the pound, written £. The pound is divided into 100 pennies (p). You can get bank notes for the following amounts – 50, 20, 10 and 5 pounds – and there are coins for £2, £1, 50, 20, 10, 5, 2 and 1p. Scotland has different bank notes from the rest of Britain, including a note for £100.

On the edge of the coins, the letters D.G.REG.F.D. always appear after the Queen's name. This stands for the Latin words *Dei Gratia Regina Fidei Defensor*, which means "By the Grace of God, Queen, Defender of the Faith".

Modern postage stamps were invented in Britain in 1840. The first was called the "Penny Black". Because Britain was the first country to have stamps, it is the only country in the world which does not have its name on them.

KEEP TO THE LEFT

In Britain, you drive on the left-hand side of the road, so the steering wheel is on the right. Britain was the first country in the world to have a "rule of the road". It was introduced to sort out the chaos on London Bridge. Keeping to the left meant that if a traveller was attacked by an oncoming rider, he wouldn't have to lean sideways across his horse to fight back with his sword or pistol.

Say it yourself!

English	Welsh	Gaelic
Welcome!	Croeso!	Fáilte!
Language	Laith	Caint
Car	Car	Gluaisteán
Money	Arian	Airgead

Around Britain

There are many different parts of Britain to visit – rich, green countryside, the hilly Lake District and Peak District, the flat Fens of East Anglia, the windswept uplands of Dartmoor and the mountainous Highlands of Scotland and Snowdonia in Wales.

Average temperatures		
Place	**January**	**July**
Edinburgh	3°C	14°C
Plymouth	6°C	16°C
Cardiff	4°C	16°C

BRITISH GEOGRAPHY

Britain's landscape is pleasant rather than spectacular. The country is generally flat and dry in the south and east, hilly and wetter towards the north and west. The highest peak in Scotland is Ben Nevis (1,343 m), in Wales, Snowdon (1,085 m) and in England, Scafell Pike (978 m). The longest rivers are the Severn (354 km), Thames (346 km) and Trent (297 km).

No part of Britain is more than 110 kilometres from the sea. Thanks to warm ocean currents in the Atlantic, Britain's climate is milder than that of its neighbours on the same latitude, such as Denmark. However, the weather is very changeable from day to day.

CANARY WHARF

London's old Docklands area has now become Europe's biggest building site as its old warehouses are converted into offices and gleaming new buildings are put up beside them. At the heart of all this is the Canary Wharf Tower – at 244 metres and 50 storeys high, it is Britain's tallest building.

THE COTSWOLDS

This upland region lies between Oxford and Bath. It is picture-postcard England at its best and a favourite day-trip for tourists from London. In the Middle Ages, the area grew rich on sheep-farming and making woollen cloth. Villages like Burford and market-towns like Bradford-on-Avon and Chipping Camden are famous for their thatched cottages, huge Gothic "wool churches" and elegant houses made of honey-coloured limestone.

THE LAKE DISTRICT

Around 1800 the dramatic landscape of this part of north-west England inspired the "Lake Poets" – Wordsworth, Coleridge and Southey. Today the area is protected as a National Park and relies heavily on tourism. The peaks around the market-town of Keswick attract climbers and hikers while lakes such as Windermere and Ullswater are popular for sailing and water-skiing. The home of the children's writer Beatrix Potter also attracts many visitors.

THE GREAT GLEN

This impressive valley is more than 96 km long and divides Scotland diagonally between north-west and south-east. Ben Nevis looms over the southern end, while historic Inverness stands at the north. Between 1803 and 1847, the Caledonian Canal was cut to link the four lochs (lakes) which lie along the Glen. This made it possible for boats to sail from the Irish Sea to the North Sea.

THE MIDLANDS

The "heart of England" is dominated by a belt of industrial cities running from Birmingham, Coventry and Wolverhampton in the west to Leicester and Nottingham in the east. But it also contains such historic treasures as Warwick Castle and Stratford-upon-Avon, the birthplace of William Shakespeare.

EAST ANGLIA AND THE FEN COUNTRY

East Anglia is made up of the three counties of Norfolk, Suffolk and Essex. The Fen country consists of marshes, drained by dykes and canals, stretching from Cambridge to Lincolnshire. Together these areas account for some of Britain's richest agricultural land. The main crops are wheat, barley, sugar beet and vegetables. The flat, silent landscape and huge cloud-filled skies were the main inspiration for England's greatest painter – John Constable.

WALES

The valleys of South Wales used to be famous for their coal-mines and steelworks. Now there are many modern electronics factories. North Wales has far fewer people, but farming and tourism are important there.

Language and Dialect

British English?

There is no such thing as a "British accent". Every part of the country has its own way of speaking English. "BBC English" is based on the speech of educated people from the south of England. Most British people can guess where someone comes from by the way they speak. Apart from accents, there are many words which are only used in a particular part of the country and are hardly heard outside it. A Yorkshire person might use the word "gradely" to describe something excellent, while a Scot would call it "braw" and a Geordie (someone from Newcastle) would say "canny".

The North

There is no single northern accent. People from Liverpool, Leeds and Newcastle all speak quite differently from one another. But there are some general differences between northern and southern English. For example, people in the south pronounce "bath" and "path" as if they were spelt "barth" and "parth". Northerners pronounce the "a" the same as in the word "cat".

Northern road signs

Southern road signs

Say it in Scots!
tae – to
wee – little
gey – very
ken – know
wadne – would not
kirk – church
bairn – child
aye – yes
burn – stream

CELTIC LANGUAGES

Welsh, Gaelic and Cornish all belong to the Celtic family of languages. Cornish, or *Kernuak*, is spoken in Cornwall. Teachers there run classes to encourage more people to use the language. Scottish Gaelic is spoken by about 69,000 people in the west of Scotland and especially on its off-shore islands. Welsh has equal status with English in Wales, which means that road signs and official forms are in both languages. Many schools teach all their lessons in Welsh and there is a Welsh TV channel. About 590,000 people speak Welsh.

Understanding Welsh Place Names
Aber – river mouth
Bryn – hill
Dol – meadow
Llan – church
Porth – harbour
Rhyd – stream/ford

FAILTE GU SGIRE
AN EILEIN SGITHEANAICH
AGUS LOCHAILLSE

WELCOME TO
SKYE & LOCHALSH

ASIAN LANGUAGES

Cities such as Bradford and Leicester have large numbers of inhabitants whose families originally came from India and Pakistan and still speak Hindi, Urdu, Punjabi and Gujarati. The Chinese communities of London and Liverpool come from around Hong Kong and speak Cantonese. In Tower Hamlets, the London docks area, the most important languages after English are Bengali and Somali.

Food and Drink

Kent is known as the "garden of England" and is famous for apples, cherries and hops. Most of Britain's fish comes through the east coast ports of Yarmouth, Hull and Grimsby. Scotland is the home of salmon and whisky, and lamb is the national dish of Wales. Laverbread (cooked seaweed) is also eaten in Wales. Cider apples come from the orchards in the south-west, from Devon to Herefordshire. Watercress is a local speciality in Hampshire. There are more than 30 different local kinds of cheese, such as Caerphilly, Wensleydale, Stilton and Red Leicester.

Outside pubs and in many seaside areas, there are often stalls selling seafood such as jellied eels and whelks or cockles. These are eaten with pepper and vinegar.

PUB GRUB

Many people eat at pubs (public houses) at lunchtimes and in the evenings. The dishes on offer usually include:

Ploughman's lunch – bread, cheese, pickles and salad.
Shepherd's pie – minced meat and vegetables topped with mashed potato and grated cheese. (This is also known as Cottage pie.)
Bangers & mash – sausages and mashed potato, often served with fried onions or baked beans.
Cornish pasty – a semi-circular pastry case stuffed with minced meat, potato and onion.
Steak & kidney pie – stewed steak and kidneys topped with crisp puff pastry. (In some tourist areas, this is often steak & mushroom pie, because some people will not eat kidneys.) Many of these dishes are eaten with English mustard – which is very hot!

For many families, the main meal of the week is Sunday lunch, perhaps roast beef with Yorkshire pudding. Take-away meals are also very popular and most towns have a selection of Indian, Italian, Chinese and Greek restaurants to choose from.

Fish and chips is the classic British take-away food. It became popular in the 1860s when railways began to bring fresh fish straight from the east coast to the great inland cities overnight. Traditionally, the fish and chips were covered with salt and malt vinegar and, using your fingers, eaten straight out of the newspaper they were wrapped in.

THE GREAT BRITISH BREAKFAST

Most people only have cereal or toast for breakfast during the week, but some still have a full cooked breakfast. A standard "full English breakfast" might consist of:

> *Cereal/Grapefruit*
>
> *Bacon and eggs (fried or scrambled)*
> *with mushrooms, beans, grilled tomatoes,*
> *fried bread, sausages*
>
> *Toast and marmalade*
>
> *Tea/Coffee/Fruit juice*

In Scotland, porridge is the traditional first course – eaten with salt, not sugar.

BEER AND WHISKY

British-style beer, made with hops, is known as "bitter". There is also a black beer with a thick, creamy head, known as "stout". This originally came from Ireland.

Whisky is the national drink of Scotland and is Britain's most valuable single export product.

Say it yourself!

English	Welsh	Gaelic
Food	Bwyd	Biadh
Breakfast	Brecwast	Biadhmaidne
Porridge	Uwd	Lite
Water	Dwr	Uisge
Egg	Wy	Ugh
Kitchen	Cegin	Tigh-cócaireachd
Lamb	Oen	Uan

A Taste of Britain

Here are some traditional recipes for you to try . . .

WELSH RAREBIT

1 Put the cheese and milk into a thick-bottomed pan. Heat it gently and keep stirring until it melts into a thick cream.

2 Add the butter, pepper, salt and mustard.

3 Raise the temperature a bit and keep stirring. The mixture should be hot, but do not let it boil.

4 Put the toast into a heatproof dish and pour the cheese mixture over it.

5 Carefully place the dish under a very hot grill until it starts to brown.

6 Remove and serve at once.

YOU WILL NEED:

100g grated cheese

25g butter

1 teaspoon mustard

⅓ cup of milk

thick-bottomed pan

heatproof dish

wooden spoon

2 slices toasted bread

pepper and salt

To make this even spicier, you could use Tabasco instead of mustard, or spread some of your favourite relish on the toast before adding the cheese.

TIME FOR TEA!

The traditional 4 o'clock tea used to consist of sandwiches, scones, fruit cake, sponge cake and dainty pastries.

MAKING TEA

Heat the water (don't fill the kettle too full!) and pour a small amount into the teapot to warm it. Swirl the water around and then throw it away. Using fresh tea, place one teaspoonful of tea for each person into the pot, and then add "one for the pot". When the water is boiling, pour it into the warmed teapot. Stir once and leave for two minutes. Pour the tea into a cup with cold milk to taste.

SCONES

YOU WILL NEED:

bowl
50g margarine
200g self-raising flour
extra flour
¼ teaspoon salt
5 table-spoons milk
baking tray
pastry board
pastry cutter (approx. 5cm in diameter)
rolling pin

SANDWICH IDEAS

Tea-time sandwiches should be dainty, and made with thinly sliced bread. Some people cut the crusts off, or cut the sandwiches into strips about 5 cm wide. Here are some ideas for fillings . . .

Cucumber Slice the cucumber very thinly. Soak it in a little vinegar for a while and drain before placing between two slices of bread.

Egg Hard-boil an egg and let it cool completely. Mash it with a little mayonnaise and pepper. You can also add finely chopped parsley or onion.

Sardine Remove any large bones. Mash and spread the fish, and add thinly sliced cucumber.

---

1 Sift the flour and salt into a bowl and rub in the margarine.

2 Gradually add the milk to make a soft dough (not too sticky!).

3 Turn out the mixture onto a board dusted with flour and roll it out until it is just over 1 cm thick.

4 Using the cutter, cut out circles until all the dough has been used up.

5 Place the circles onto a baking tray which has been lightly greased with margarine.

6 Bake in the oven at 400°F/200°C/Gas mark 6 for about 12 to 14 minutes. The scones should be lightly golden in colour and firm to the touch.

How to serve

1 After baking, set the scones aside to cool and harden a little.

2 Cut in half. Spread with butter, then add some jam, and top it off with some fresh whipped or clotted cream. Delicious!

Say it yourself!

English	Welsh	Gaelic
Butter	Menyn	Ìm
Milk	Llaeth	Bainne
Bread	Bara	Aran
Cheese	Caws	Cáis
Soup	Cawl	Eanaraich
Cake	Cacen	Breacag

Life in Britain

WHERE PEOPLE LIVE

About 90 per cent of British people live in towns and cities. Almost one in four live within 25 km of London. The next biggest cities are Birmingham, with a population of 1.2 million people, and Leeds with over 700,000 people. Many people live in houses with gardens, while others live in high-rise tower blocks. Single-storey bungalows are popular with retired people, many of whom often live along the south coast or in the south-west of England where the weather is usually milder.

Many people would like to live in villages, but it often costs too much to travel to work, school and shops. Some of the smaller, pretty villages make money from selling teas, souvenirs and antiques to summer visitors. Traditionally there are two main types of village – the "long street", where all the buildings are placed beside the main road, and the "nucleated", where the houses are all clustered around a central point, such as the village green, pond, church or inn.

WHAT PEOPLE DO

British agriculture is highly mechanised and efficient, so it doesn't need many workers. Major industries include making machinery, cars, aircraft, chemicals and electronic goods. Most people work in offices, shops, schools or hospitals. The fastest-growing businesses are banking and tourism.

POLICE

There is no national police force in Britain. Instead, each county or major city has its own. There is also a separate force for the railways. The biggest police force is London's Metropolitan Police. The emergency telephone number for the police, and the other emergency services, is 999.

14

GOING TO SCHOOL

British children have to go to school from the age of five until they are 16. Over 90 per cent go to state schools, where the education is paid for out of taxes. Some children go to independent schools for which their parents have to pay. These include some of the country's oldest and most famous boarding-schools, such as Eton College which is over 500 years old. Some schools make pupils wear a uniform, and you can also find schools which will only take boys or girls. Those schools which take both, regardless of their abilities, are known as comprehensive schools. There are over 100 universities in Britain, the oldest being Oxford and Cambridge.

KEEPING INFORMED

Because Britain is quite a small country, you can buy the same newspaper in every part of the country, although local editions will carry different sports news and advertisemments. There are also many local newspapers.

The British Broadcasting Corporation (BBC) controls two terrestrial TV channels and a number of digital ones. BBC Radio runs five main national radio networks and the World Service, which broadcasts in over 30 languages. Independent Television (ITV) has two terrestrial TV channels, with another operated separately. Satellite TV is also available .

SHOPPING

In Britain you can find Europe's largest shopping mall – the Metro Centre at Gateshead in the north-east of England. London has such famous department stores as Harrod's and Selfridge's as well as specialist shops like Hamleys (toys) and Virgin Megastore (CDs, videos and games). The most famous high-street chainstores are Marks & Spencer, W H Smith and Boots. But old-fashioned open-air markets are still very popular in both towns and villages.

Say it yourself!

English	Welsh	Gaelic
Police	Heddlu	Riaghladh Baile
School	Ysgol	Sgoil
Shop	Siop	Bùth
Market	Marchnad	Margadh
Work	Gwaith	Obair

Dressing the Part

The formal male attire of a suit with matching jacket, waistcoat and trousers is an English invention, as are the blazer and the bowler hat. London's Savile Row is the home of the world's best tailoring. Nearby Jermyn Street is where a gentleman gets his shirts and shoes made to measure, while younger people like to look in the shops in the King's Road, Chelsea, for the latest fashions.

Designers such as Mary Quant, Zandra Rhodes, Vivienne Westwood and Bruce Oldfield have revolutionised Britain's standing in the world of high fashion.

THE CITY GENT

The true "City Gent" is not such a common sight today, but he still represents many people's idea of the "typical Englishman".

SCOTTISH SPLENDOUR

North of the border, you may come across men wearing kilts, usually for some ceremonial purpose. The tartan pattern worn depends on which clan (family) you belong to or which army regiment you have served in.

Each year famous designers take part in London Fashion Week. They show off their latest fashion designs.

WELSH WOOLLENS

The traditional dress worn by Welsh women to an Eisteddfod (see page 25) is based on the fashions of the 17th century when housewives working at home would wear their woollen bed-gown and an apron on top of a petticoat. When they went out, they would add a shawl and hat and, in winter, a hooded cloak.

BE A PEARLY!

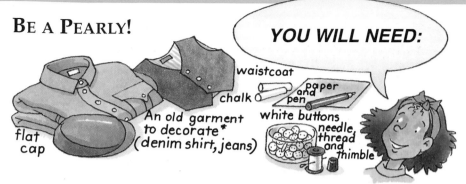

waistcoat

chalk

YOU WILL NEED:

paper and pen

white buttons

needle, thread and thimble

An old garment to decorate* (denim shirt, jeans)

flat cap

1 Draw your design first on paper and then copy this onto your garment with the chalk.

2 Following your pattern, sew the buttons on quite firmly.

3 Put on the waistcoat or jacket and the flat cap, and you have your own "pearly" outfit.

PEARLY KINGS AND QUEENS

At the beginning of this century, most Londoners bought their fruit and vegetables from street-markets. The stall-holders were known as "costermongers" or "barrow boys". Costers had their own special language and dressed up to look really "pie and mash" (= "flash" = smart).

Costers liked to decorate their waistcoats with bright buttons made of brass or, better still, pearl. And the more buttons, the better. Soon every district of London's East End had its own "Pearly King and Queen". The "title" was passed down in families and they still exist today, although they only dress up in their full regalia to raise money for charity.

Say it yourself!

English	Welsh	Gaelic
Shirt	Crys	Léine
Shoe	Esgid	Brôg
Hat	Het	Biorraid
Trousers	Trowsus	Triubhas
Jacket	Siaced	Seacaid

Made in Britain

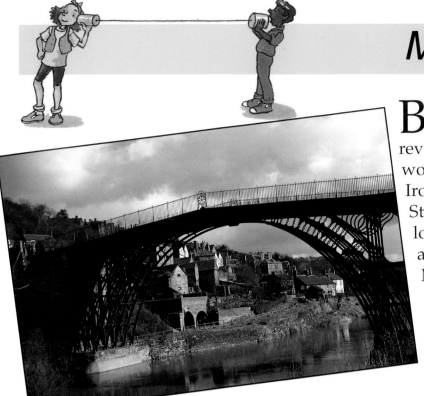

Britain was the first country in the world to have an industrial revolution. The first iron bridge in the world (built in 1779) can be found at Ironbridge in central England. George Stephenson's famous steam locomotive, *Rocket*, was built in 1829, and is now on show at the Science Museum in London. It was the first reliable locomotive of its kind.

Here are some other important moments in British science and technology:

1687 Newton formulates laws of gravity and planetary motion.

1712 The first successful steam engine, the Dudley Castle Newcomen, is built.

1825 The first public railway is opened between Stockton and Darlington in the north of England.

1863 The world's first underground railway opens in London.

1876 The telephone is invented by Alexander Graham Bell.

1928 Alexander Fleming accidentally discovers penicillin, the first antibiotic.

1955 The hovercraft is patented.

1978 The world's first test-tube baby is born.

1994 The Channel Tunnel is opened, linking Britain and France.

Comet and Concorde

In 1919 two British pilots, Alcock and Brown, became the first men to fly the Atlantic in a British-built Vickers Vimy bomber. In 1930, inventor Frank Whittle patented a design for the first jet engine. In 1952, Britain became the first country to introduce regular jet passenger services in the De Havilland Comet. The Anglo-French Concorde, the world's first supersonic airliner, has been flying the Atlantic in three hours since 1976.

North Sea Oil and Gas

Gas was discovered under the North Sea in 1965 and oil in 1969. By 1977, almost all the gas used in Britain was coming from the North Sea and by 1994 Britain had become the ninth largest oil producer in the world. The drilling rigs used to explore for oil and gas and then pump them ashore have to be able to stand up to winds of 260 km/h and waves 30 m high.

The Best Car in the World

Britain is the home of the names of many historic high-performance car manufacturers, such as Aston-Martin, Austin-Healy, Lotus, M.G., Bentley and Jaguar. Rolls Royce is the one name that outshines them all.

In 1904, Mr F. H. Royce, an engineer, met the Honourable C. S. Rolls, a car salesman. At the 1906 Motor Show they launched the Rolls Royce *Silver Ghost*. It had polished aluminium bodywork and real silver fittings. They put it on an endurance test to show that it was more than just beautiful to look at. It ran for 14,371 miles without a fault – doubling the previous record. The Rolls Royce record stood for more than 50 years, proving that the *Silver Ghost* was indeed the best car in the world.

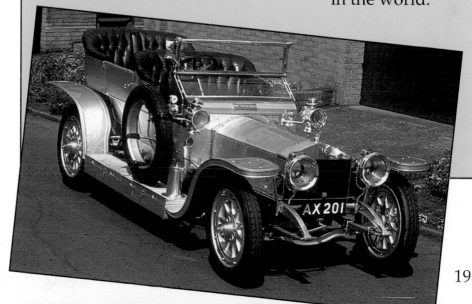

Sport

Sport is Britain's gift to the world. Cricket, soccer, rugby, tennis, squash, table tennis, badminton, canoeing and snooker were all invented in Britain. The first rules for such sports as boxing, golf, hockey, yachting and horse-racing also originated from Britain. The most popular sports that people take part in, rather than watching, are angling, snooker and darts.

FOOTBALL

Football began as a contest between neighbouring villages – with no limit to the number on each side, no fixed pitch and almost no rules! The Football Association drew up the rules of the modern game in 1863 and in 1888 12 clubs joined together to form the first Football League. England won the World Cup in 1966. English teams such as Tottenham Hotspur, Arsenal, Liverpool and Manchester United have fans all around the world.

CRICKET

Cricket is very much the English game. At village level, a match can be played in an afternoon. At international level it can take five days – and still end in a draw. A form of cricket was being played 250 years ago. The first Australian team to visit England came in 1882 – and won!

HIGHLAND GAMES

Over 70 Highland Games meetings are held in Scotland each year. The most famous take place at Braemar in Aberdeenshire, Scotland in September and are attended by the Royal family. Events include throwing the hammer and tossing the caber (a pole 6 m long, weighing over 50 kg).

RUGBY

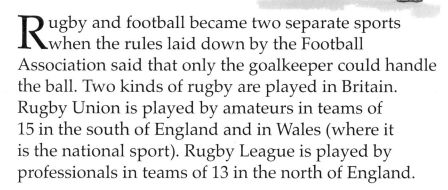

Rugby and football became two separate sports when the rules laid down by the Football Association said that only the goalkeeper could handle the ball. Two kinds of rugby are played in Britain. Rugby Union is played by amateurs in teams of 15 in the south of England and in Wales (where it is the national sport). Rugby League is played by professionals in teams of 13 in the north of England.

GOLF

Golf was probably invented in Holland, but has been played in Scotland for at least 400 years. At first, it was played with balls made of wood, then of leather stuffed with feathers. The earliest rules were drawn up in 1754 at the Royal and Ancient course in St Andrews.

TENNIS

Tennis was originally called "sphairistike"! The first rules were drawn up by the All-England Lawn Tennis and Croquet Club when it held its first tournament in the London suburb of Wimbledon in 1877. Wimbledon is still the world's most famous tennis event.

Play the Game!

DOMINOES

This is a traditional game played in pubs. Dominoes are normally made of wood or plastic but you can make your own out of thick card, marking the dots as shown below with felt-tip pen. You will also need to bend some long pieces of card to make racks so that you can see your own dominoes without letting your opponent see them.

There are many different ways of playing the game. This is one of the simplest.

1 Place the 28 domino cards face down on a table and mix them up.

There are two basic versions. You will need 1 large button or counter and 6 small ones. It is best to play on a hard, smooth surface like a piece of board.

Version 1

1 Draw two parallel lines 1 metre apart to make a start and finish line.

2 Each player has 3 small buttons and takes it in turn to use the large one to press firmly on the edge of the small buttons. This should make them jump forward.

3 The aim is to be the first to get 3 buttons behind the finish line.

2 Each player picks up one card. The one with the highest number of points gets to pick up the rest of their cards first and to start the game. Replace the two "draw" domino cards and mix them all up again.

3 Each player takes it in turn to pick up 14 cards each.

4 The first player lays down a card. Suppose it has 5 dots and 1 dot on it. The next player can put down either a domino with 5 dots on, or one with 1 dot. If you can't go, you knock on the table and lose a turn.

5 Dominoes with two matching figures on (3 + 3) are laid sideways across the line. To continue from this, you need another card with a 3 on it.

6 The game usually ends when one player has managed to use up all their dominoes. If you end up with everyone not being able to go, add up the number of dots on the dominoes still held. The winner is the one with the lowest score.

Version 2

Instead of drawing 2 parallel lines, draw 3 or 4 circles one inside the other. Each ring can be given a different score. You can put an egg-cup in the "bulls'-eye" and give the highest score for getting the button into the cup.

You can make up your own versions of tiddlywinks. Some people play it blindfolded!

British Bobby

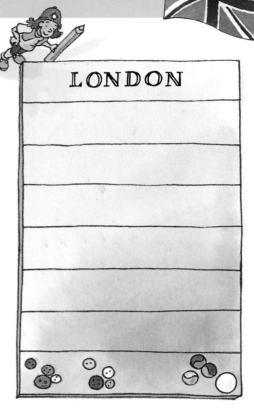

This is a children's version of the game "shove ha'penny". You will need a large piece of thick paper (120 x 80 cm) and a crayon. Mark the card into 8 equal parts. Label the last one "London".

You can play this with buttons on a table-top, or with a marble or table-tennis ball on the floor.

1 Players take it in turn to slide the button/roll the marble/blow the ball from the edge of the paper farthest from "London".

2 If the button/marble/ball stops safely between two lines, you can draw the outline of a policeman's helmet and write your name inside it.

If it stops on a line or goes over the edge, there is no score. If it stops in "London", the player takes another turn.

3 The winner is the first one to get a helmet in five of the spaces, with no gaps between them.

Holidays and Festivals

More than a third of the population takes a foreign holiday each year. The main attraction is the guaranteed sunshine of the Mediterranean, and the most popular destinations are Spain, France and Greece.

THEME PARKS

Purpose-built leisure attractions are quite new in Britain but there are now more than 100 to be found. Alton Towers and Thorpe Park are like a giant fun-fair, while the Jorvik Centre re-creates what York was like in Viking times, even down to the smells. In Manchester you can tour the studios of Granada Television.

THE SEASIDE

The idea that sea-bathing is good for you dates from about 1820. Brighton was the first seaside resort. Later railways made it possible for people to take cheap day-trips to the coast. Piers were built so that people could walk out to sea and breathe in the salty air. There are seaside resorts all around the coast. The biggest one is Blackpool.

STATELY HOMES

The British love visiting old houses and castles – and there are thousands to choose from. Longleat, Chatsworth and Blenheim Palace are some of the most famous. The most spectacular castles are in Wales (Caernarfon, Conway) and along the border between England and Scotland (Alnwick, Bamburgh).

MUSEUMS

There are many different kinds of museums in Britain. London alone has more than 200, including museums about artillery, scouts, nursing, films and TV, design, ships and the sea, the theatre, transport, toys and musical instruments.

MAY DAY

The first day of May used to be a holiday to celebrate the coming of spring. People would go "maying" in the woods and collect green branches and blossom to decorate their houses. A Maypole was put up to dance around and a young girl was chosen as "May Queen" to head a procession through the village or town. These celebrations are still held in different parts of England.

GUY FAWKES

On 5 November, people light bonfires and let off fireworks in memory of Guy Fawkes who tried to blow up Parliament with barrels of gunpowder in 1605. Sometimes a "guy" made up of old clothes is burned on the fire.

BURNS NIGHT

On 25 January each year, some Scots hold banquets in honour of Robert Burns, Scotland's national poet. He wrote the words of "Auld Lang Syne", a song traditionally sung at New Year.

The main course of the banquet is usually a haggis, which is chopped meat, spices and vegetables, all cooked in a sheep's stomach. It is carried to the table with great honour, accompanied by a Highland piper. It is served with "tatties" (potatoes) and "bashed neeps" (mashed turnips). The poet's health is toasted in whisky.

NOTTING HILL CARNIVAL

The idea of a street carnival came to Britain from Trinidad. For 40 years, a carnival has been organised by Afro-Caribbean people living in Notting Hill, west London. It is held on the last weekend in August, and attracts 1 million people on the first day alone, making it Europe's largest street event.

HOGMANAY

In Scotland, the New Year celebrations (Hogmanay) are even more important than Christmas. At midnight, people go "first footing" and visit the homes of friends with gifts which traditionally include a lump of coal and a silver coin.

EISTEDDFOD

Eisteddfod is the Welsh name for a festival of music, poetry, drama and handicrafts. They have been held for over 1,000 years. The most important is the Royal National Eisteddfod which is held every August. The Welsh language is spoken in all the events.

The Arts

GREAT WRITERS

Britain is probably best known for its literature. Many of the characters created by British writers are well known even in countries that do not speak English as their main language. These include Robin Hood, Sherlock Holmes, James Bond, Winnie the Pooh, and Peter Rabbit. English poetry is also well known, through the works of such poets as Keats, Shelley, Byron and Browning.

British Winners of the Nobel Prize for Literature

1907	Rudyard Kipling
1932	John Galsworthy
1948	T. S. Eliot
1950	Bertrand Russell
1953	Sir Winston Churchill
1983	William Golding

William Shakespeare (1564–1616)

Shakespeare is probably the world's most famous playwright. He wrote 37 plays, including *Hamlet* and *Romeo and Juliet*. Shakespeare also acted in plays and was one of the owners of a theatre called the Globe. This has been rebuilt in London so that people can see how plays were acted in his day – in daylight, and open to the sky!

Charles Dickens (1812–70)

Shakespeare's Globe Theatre stood on the south bank of the Thames.

Sir Christopher Wren rebuilt St. Paul's between 1675 and 1710.

In his novels, Dickens invented such characters as Oliver Twist and Mr Pickwick. When he was young, Dickens wanted to be an actor. After he became famous, he used to give public readings from his books. He is buried in "Poets' Corner" in Westminster Abbey. A portrait of Dickens appears on the £10 bank-note.

Dylan Thomas (1914–53)

Dylan Thomas was a Welsh poet who wrote in English. His most famous poem is *Under Milk Wood* which describes the people of a Welsh seaside village.

DESIGN

Sir Christopher Wren (1632–1723)

Sir Christopher Wren helped to rebuild London after the Great Fire of 1666. His most famous building is St Paul's Cathedral, but he also designed over 50 churches.

MUSIC TODAY

In Wales there are competitions for male voice choirs and some in the north of England for brass bands. In Scotland, the bands feature drums, flutes and bagpipes.

The composer Sir Edward Elgar (1857–1934) is well known for ceremonial music such as *Pomp and Circumstance,* and for choral/orchestral works. Many music societies also perform the comic operas composed by Sir William Gilbert (1836–1911) and Sir Arthur Sullivan (1842–1900), one of the most popular being *The Mikado.*

Britain's most famous modern composer is Benjamin Britten (1913–76). He started a famous annual music festival at Aldeburgh in Suffolk.

ART

English painting was at its best between 1750 and 1850. John Constable (1776–1837) and Joseph Turner (1775–1851) were both excellent landscape painters.

John Constable painted scenes of the Suffolk countryside. He sketched outdoors in summer and painted in his studio in winter.

Josiah Wedgwood (1730-95)

Wedgwood pottery is famous around the world. Many of the designs are based on carvings from ancient Greece and Rome.

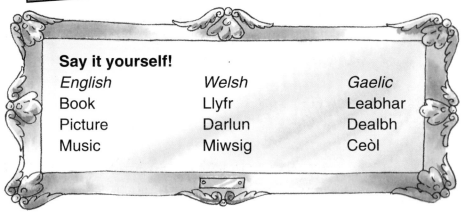

Say it yourself!

English	Welsh	Gaelic
Book	Llyfr	Leabhar
Picture	Darlun	Dealbh
Music	Miwsig	Ceòl

British History

Britain is steeped with history. Here are just a few of the key events.

THE ENGLISH

The ancestors of the modern English are the Angles, Saxons and Jutes. They came from the area where Germany, Holland and Denmark now meet. They began to settle in England from the 5th century AD and drove the native British into Wales. During Anglo-Saxon times, England was raided by Vikings from Denmark and Norway. In the end many of them came to settle, too. Most villages in England got their names from the Anglo-Saxons or the Vikings.

THE ROMANS

The Roman conquest of Britain began in 43 AD. Roman rule lasted for almost 400 years. They founded London, York, Lincoln and Chester, but they never conquered Scotland. On the orders of the Emperor Hadrian, they built a wall right across the country to stop Scottish raids.

THE NORMANS

In 1066, England was invaded by Normans (Vikings who had settled in France). The last Anglo-Saxon king, Harold, was completely defeated at the Battle of Hastings. The Normans built many castles, and French became the language of the rulers until about 1400. Many French words were added to the English language.

ELIZABETH I (1558–1603)

Many people think that Elizabeth I was England's greatest ruler. She was very hard-working and spoke French, Italian, Greek, Latin and Welsh. In 1588, her navy defeated the great Armada sent by Spain to conquer England.

EMPIRE

In 1607, English people founded Jamestown in Virginia and began to settle in America. Although the American colonies became independent after 1776, Britain's empire continued to grow until it became the biggest in the history of the world. The colony with the biggest population was India. The biggest in area were Canada and Australia.

	Time Band
43 AD	Roman conquest begins.
871-99	Alfred the Great reconquers England from the Vikings.
1066	The Norman conquest.
1215	King John signs the Magna Carta
1485	Tudor victory at Bosworth ends the "Wars of the Roses".
1536	Henry VIII makes himself the head of the Church of England.
1603	James VI of Scotland becomes King of England as well.
1666	Great Fire of London destroys a major part of the city.
1707	Act of Union joins England and Scotland under one Parliament.
1805	Nelson wins the Battle of Trafalgar.
1837-1901	Reign of Queen Victoria; Britain becomes leading world power.
1939-1945	World War II.
1947	Independence of India signals the end of the British Empire.
1973	Britain joins the European Community (now the European Union).
2002	Commonwealth Games held in Britain.

INDUSTRIAL REVOLUTION

Britain was the first country to develop industries based on steam-power and organised factories. In 1851, a "Great Exhibition" was held in Hyde Park in London to show off Britain's industrial power. This was the world's first international fair.

SIR WINSTON CHURCHILL (1874-1965)

Churchill was the most famous Englishman of the 20th century. As a young man he was an army officer who fought in India and Africa. Then he went into politics and was a great public speaker. He was Prime Minister from 1940 to 1945 (during World War II), and again from 1951 to 1955. He also wrote many history books and won the Nobel Prize for Literature.

Say it yourself!

English	Welsh	Gaelic
History	Hanes	Eachdraidh
King	Brenin	Rîgh
Battle	Brwdyr	Cath
Castle	Castel	Daingneach

Round Britain Race

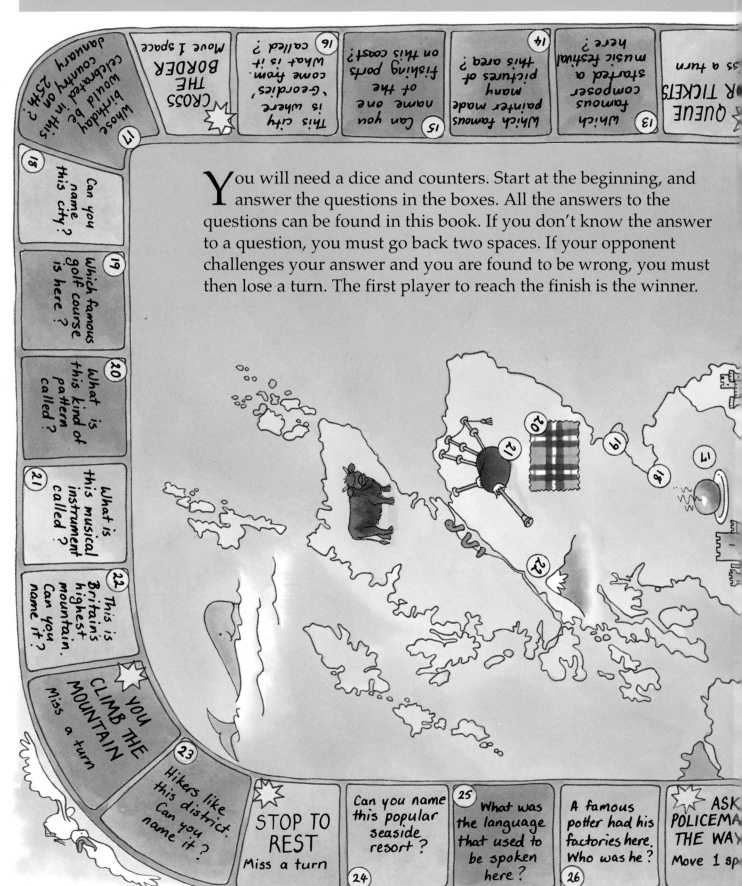

You will need a dice and counters. Start at the beginning, and answer the questions in the boxes. All the answers to the questions can be found in this book. If you don't know the answer to a question, you must go back two spaces. If your opponent challenges your answer and you are found to be wrong, you must then lose a turn. The first player to reach the finish is the winner.

12 Can you name the tennis tournament held here?

11 What is the name of the giant skyscraper built here?

10 Can you name the festival held here in August?

9 Can you name this river?

8 What kinds of foods is this country famous for?

7 You can cross to France here on a British invention.

6 This is the county called of England. It's 'garden'. What is its name?

TAKE THE FERRY
Move 1 space

5 Can you name this island?

4 This area is popular with tourists. Can you name it?

3 Can you name the kind of cheese made here?

2 What drink is made here.

1 What is this kind of snack called?

28 What is the National Anthem of this country?

29 What does the flag of this country look like?

30 What is this mountainous region called?

31 Can you name this city?

Shakespeare was born here. What is this town called?

HOME

START

Index

Additional photographs:
Bridgeman cover, P. 26, 27, 28. Camera Press P. 29. J. Allan Cash Ltd P. 10, 15, cover. Eye Ubiquitous P. 6, 9, 14, 15, 28, cover. Chris Fairclough P. 7, 9, 14. Robert Harding cover, p. 17, 18, 24, 25. P. MacDonald P. 7. Frank Spooner P. 8. Sporting Pictures (UK) Ltd: 20c. Ray Tang/Rex Features: 16t. Zefa P. 7, 19.